LAUNCH YOUR ONLINE FASHION BUSINESS: A GUIDE TO SUCCESS

TUSHAR RAJ

Made with ❤ on the Notion Press Platform
www.notionpress.com

To the dreamers and risk-takers, the go-getters, and the game-changers, this guide is dedicated to you. You are the ones who dare to chase your passions, turn your ideas into reality, and create something that makes a difference in the world.

Starting an online fashion business can be a daunting task, but with hard work, determination, and the proper knowledge, it can also be incredibly rewarding. This guide is here to help you on your journey, and to provide you with the tools and resources you need to succeed.

We dedicate this guide to all entrepreneurs who are willing to put in the time and effort to make their dreams a reality. To the ones who are not afraid to fail, but embrace each challenge as an opportunity to learn and grow.

So here's to you, the trailblazers, the innovators, the fashion-forward thinkers. May this guide be a source of inspiration and guidance as you embark on your entrepreneurial journey and launch your online fashion business.

Contents

Foreword *vii*

Preface *ix*

Acknowledgements *xi*

Prologue *xiii*

Author Info *xv*

1. Introduction 1
2. Research And Planning 3
3. Setting Up Your E-commerce Platform 6
4. Building Your Product Line 9
5. Marketing And Promotion 12
6. Growing Your Business 14
7. Conclusion 16
8. References And Resources 18

Foreword

Welcome to "Launch Your Online Fashion Business: A Guide to Success"! If you're reading this, it's likely that you're interested in starting your own online fashion business and making your dream a reality. Starting a business can be an exciting but overwhelming journey, and it's important to have a clear plan and direction in place to help you achieve your goals.

This guide is here to help you every step of the way. Whether you're a seasoned entrepreneur or a fashion enthusiast with a passion for design, this guide is packed with practical advice and actionable steps to help you turn your vision into a thriving online fashion business.

From developing your brand identity to setting up your website, marketing your products and managing your finances, we cover it all. You'll learn about the different challenges you'll face and how to overcome them, as well as valuable tips for growing your business and expanding your customer base.

This guide is written in a friendly, approachable tone and is designed to be easy to follow, even if you have no prior experience in business. We understand that starting a business can be daunting, but with the right tools and resources, anyone can make their dream a reality.

So, let's get started! Whether you're ready to take the plunge and start your business today, or you're just starting to explore the possibilities, this guide is the perfect place to begin. We can't wait to see the amazing fashion business you'll create!

Sincerely,
Tushar Raj

Preface

Dear Fashion Enthusiast,

Congratulations on taking the first step toward launching your own online fashion business! Launching an online fashion business can be an exciting, yet challenging journey, but with the right guidance, it can be a huge success. This guide is designed to be your go-to resource for everything you need to know about launching a successful online fashion business.

In this guide, you'll learn the key steps and strategies for launching your online fashion business, from developing your business plan and choosing the right products to set up your online store and marketing your brand. We'll also cover important topics like pricing, customer service, and branding to help you get your business off the ground and running smoothly.

Whether you're a seasoned entrepreneur or just starting out, this guide is packed with practical tips and advice to help you achieve your goals. We'll share the successes and failures of some of the industry's most successful fashion entrepreneurs, and provide you with the tools and resources you need to overcome any challenges you may face along the way.

So, roll up your sleeves and get ready to embark on an exciting journey to launch your own online fashion business! With this guide in hand, you'll be well on your way to reaching your goals and becoming a successful fashion entrepreneur.

Best of luck

Acknowledgements

The journey to launch a successful online fashion business is not an easy one, and it is with immense gratitude that we acknowledge the many individuals who have helped us along the way.

First and foremost, we would like to thank our families for their unwavering support and encouragement throughout the creation of this guide. Your love and belief in us have been a constant source of inspiration and motivation.

We would also like to extend our appreciation to the fashion industry experts who have generously shared their knowledge and experience with us. Your insights have been invaluable and have helped to make this guide as comprehensive and useful as possible.

Additionally, we would like to acknowledge the hard work and dedication of our team at OpenAI. Without your expertise in artificial intelligence and natural language processing, this guide would not have been possible.

Finally, we would like to thank our readers for choosing "Launch Your Online Fashion Business: A Guide to Success". It is our hope that this guide will empower you to turn your fashion business dreams into a reality.

With gratitude,

TR GROUP TEAM

Prologue

Congratulations on taking the first step toward launching your online fashion business! The world of fashion is constantly evolving, and the rise of e-commerce has opened up new opportunities for fashion entrepreneurs. With the right strategy, you can build a thriving online fashion business that reaches customers all over the world.

This guide has been designed to take you through the key steps of launching your online fashion business, from researching your target market to setting up your e-commerce platform, and everything in between. Whether you're a seasoned entrepreneur or just starting out, you'll find practical advice and tips to help you succeed.

The fashion industry can be competitive, but it's also incredibly rewarding. By creating a unique brand and delivering high-quality products and services, you can establish a loyal customer base and build a successful business. With hard work and determination, you can turn your passion for fashion into a profitable venture.

So let's get started! This guide is your roadmap to success, and it's filled with the information and resources you need to make your online fashion business a reality. Get ready to unleash your style and take your place in the fashion world!

Author Info

Tushar Raj

Author

CHAPTER ONE

Introduction

Welcome to the world of online fashion! This exciting and dynamic industry offers a wealth of opportunities for entrepreneurs who are passionate about fashion and have a vision for success. In this chapter, we'll provide an overview of the online fashion industry and explore the benefits of launching an online fashion business.

A. Overview of the Online Fashion Industry

The online fashion industry has exploded in recent years, with e-commerce sales reaching new heights each year. Consumers are increasingly turning to the internet to buy clothes, shoes, accessories, and more, and this trend shows no signs of slowing down. With the right strategy, you can tap into this growing market and build a successful online fashion business.

B. Benefits of Launching an Online Fashion Business

There are many benefits to launching an online fashion business, including:

1. Lower start-up costs: Compared to opening a brick-and-mortar store, starting an online fashion business can be less expensive. You'll still need to invest in a website, product inventory, and marketing, but you won't have the overhead costs of a physical location.

2. Increased reach: With an online store, you can reach customers all over the world. This means you can sell your products to a much larger audience than you would with a brick-and-mortar store.

3. Flexibility: Running an online fashion business allows you to work from anywhere and set your own schedule. You can manage your store from your laptop, phone, or tablet, making it easier to balance work and life.

4. Access to data: Running an online business provides you with valuable data about your customers and their buying habits. You can use this information to make informed decisions about product development, marketing, and sales.

5. Build a brand: With an online store, you have the opportunity to build a strong brand and establish yourself as an expert in your field. You can use your website, social media, and other marketing channels to tell your story and build relationships with your customers.

In conclusion, launching an online fashion business can be a lucrative and rewarding venture. With the right strategy, you can turn your passion for fashion into a profitable business that reaches customers all over the world. The next chapters of this guide will provide the information and resources you need to make your dream a reality.

CHAPTER TWO

Research and Planning

The research and planning stage is a critical step in launching your online fashion business. In this chapter, you'll learn how to define your target market, conduct market research, and develop a business plan. You'll also learn how to create a unique brand that sets you apart from the competition.

A. Defining Your Target Market

Your target market is the group of people who are most likely to buy your products. To define your target market, you'll need to consider factors such as age, gender, income, and lifestyle. Ask yourself questions like:

1. Who is most likely to buy my products?
2. What are their needs and wants?
3. Where do they shop and what brands do they prefer?

Once you have a clear understanding of your target market, you'll be able to tailor your products, marketing, and customer service to meet their needs.

B. Conducting Market Research

Market research is the process of gathering information about your target market, competitors, and industry trends. There are many different ways to conduct market research, including:

1. Surveys and questionnaires

2. Focus groups
3. Competitor analysis
4. Industry reports

Market research will help you understand your customers, identify gaps in the market, and make informed decisions about your business strategy.

C. Developing a Business Plan

A business plan is a roadmap that outlines your goals, strategies, and tactics for launching and growing your business. Your business plan should include:

1. An executive summary
2. A description of your products and services
3. A market analysis
4. A description of your target market
5. A marketing and sales strategy
6. A financial plan
7. A business plan will help you stay focused and on track as you launch your online fashion business.

D. Creating a Unique Brand

Your brand is what sets you apart from the competition and helps you connect with your target market. To create a unique brand, you'll need to consider factors such as:

1. Your brand name
2. Your brand logo
3. Your brand values and personality
4. Your brand messaging and tone of voice

By creating a unique brand, you'll be able to establish a strong identity and build a loyal customer base.

In conclusion, the research and planning stage is an important step in launching your online fashion business. By defining your target market, conducting market research, developing a business plan, and creating a unique brand, you'll be well on your way to success. So take the time to do your research, and make sure you have a solid foundation before you move on to the next stage.

CHAPTER THREE

Setting Up Your E-Commerce Platform

Setting up your e-commerce platform is an essential step in launching your online fashion business. Your e-commerce platform will be the foundation of your online store, and it's where you'll sell your products and interact with customers. In this chapter, we'll cover the key steps to help you get your platform up and running.

A. Choosing an E-Commerce Platform

There are many e-commerce platforms to choose from, and each one offers different features and benefits. When choosing a platform, it's important to consider the following factors:

1. Cost: Some platforms are free to use, while others charge a monthly or transaction fee.
2. Ease of use: Choose a platform that's user-friendly and easy to navigate.
3. Customization: Look for a platform that allows you to customize the look and feel of your website.
4. Integration: Consider a platform that integrates with the tools and services you already use, such as payment processors and shipping providers.

5. Scalability: Choose a platform that can grow with your business, and that offers the features you need as your business expands.

Popular e-commerce platforms include Shopify, WooCommerce, BigCommerce, and Magento. You can read more about each platform, and compare their features, on their respective websites.

B. Designing Your Website

Once you've chosen an e-commerce platform, it's time to design your website. Your website is your online storefront, and it's where customers will come to shop for your products. It's important to create a website that's professional, easy to use, and aesthetically pleasing. Here are some tips to help you design a great website:

Keep it simple: Use a clean and simple layout, and avoid clutter.

1. Make it easy to navigate: Organize your products into categories, and make it easy for customers to find what they're looking for.

2. Showcase your products: Use high-quality images and descriptions to showcase your products and their features.

3. Be mobile-friendly: Make sure your website is optimized for mobile devices, as more and more customers shop on their smartphones.

4. Include customer reviews: Encourage customers to leave reviews of your products, and display those reviews prominently on your website.

C. Building Your Online Store

Once you've designed your website, it's time to build your online store. Your online store is where you'll list your products, process orders, and manage your inventory. Here are some tips to help you build a great online store:

1. List your products: Use high-quality images and descriptions to showcase your products, and make sure the information is accurate and up-to-date.

2. Make checkout easy: Make it easy for customers to complete their purchases, and include a secure checkout process.

3. Offer various payment options: Offer a range of payment options, such as credit cards, PayPal, and others.

4. Manage your inventory: Keep track of your inventory levels, and make sure you have enough stock to meet customer demand.

D. Setting Up Payment and Shipping Options

Finally, you'll need to set up payment and shipping options for your online store. Your payment options will determine how customers pay for your products, and your shipping options will determine how you get your products to customers. Here are some tips to help you set up payment and shipping options:

1. Choose a payment processor: Choose a payment processor that's secure, reliable, and integrates with your e-commerce platform.

2. Set up shipping options: Choose a shipping provider and set

CHAPTER FOUR

Building Your Product Line

When it comes to building your product line, the options are endless. From trendy clothing and accessories to unique and statement pieces, the world of fashion is full of possibilities. However, the key to success is having a well-thought-out product line that meets the needs and desires of your target market.

A. Sourcing and Manufacturing Your Products

One of the first decisions you'll need to make is how you will source and manufacture your products. You have several options to choose from, including:

1. Designing and manufacturing your own products: If you have experience in fashion design, this can be a great way to create unique, high-quality products that set you apart from the competition. However, this can also be time-consuming and expensive.

2. Working with a manufacturer: Another option is to work with a manufacturer to produce your products. This allows you to focus on the design and marketing of your products, while the manufacturer handles the production process.

3. Dropshipping: Dropshipping is a fulfillment method where you don't keep any physical inventory. Instead, you work with a supplier who ships products directly to your customers on your behalf. This can be a cost-effective solution, but you may have less control over the quality of your products and the shipping process.

Whichever option you choose, it's important to carefully research and select a reliable and high-quality supplier or manufacturer who can meet your needs and deliver products that meet your standards.

B. Building a Strong Product Line

Once you've decided on your sourcing and manufacturing options, it's time to build your product line. When creating your product line, consider the following:

1. Your target market: What are the needs and desires of your target market? What kind of products do they want and what sets your brand apart from others?

2. Trends and competition: Stay up-to-date on fashion trends and be aware of what your competitors are offering. Use this information to create a product line that stands out.

3. Quality and uniqueness: Ensure that your products are high-quality and unique. This will help to build trust and loyalty with your customers.

4. Diversity: Offer a range of products in different styles, colors, and sizes to cater to a wide range of customers.

C. Pricing Your Products

Pricing your products is an important aspect of building your product line. You want to ensure that your prices are competitive, while still allowing you to make a profit. When determining your pricing, consider the following:

1. Cost of goods: Consider the cost of manufacturing, shipping, and other expenses associated with producing

your products.

2. Market prices: Research the prices of similar products in the market to ensure that your prices are competitive.

3. Brand value: Consider the value of your brand and the quality of your products when setting your prices.

4. Profit margins: Determine your desired profit margins and adjust your prices accordingly.

D. Staying on Top of Trends

The fashion industry is constantly evolving, and it's important to stay up-to-date on the latest trends. This can be achieved by:

1. Following fashion blogs and websites: Keep an eye on fashion blogs and websites to stay informed about the latest trends.

2. Attending fashion events: Attend fashion events and trade shows to see the latest collections and get inspiration for your own product line.

3. Keeping in touch with customers: Ask your customers for feedback and suggestions on what they'd like to see in your product line.

By staying on top of trends

CHAPTER FIVE

Marketing and Promotion

Marketing and promotion are critical components of any successful online fashion business. By building a strong online presence and reaching out to your target market, you can attract customers, generate sales, and grow your business. In this chapter, we'll cover the key steps of building an effective marketing and promotion strategy for your online fashion business.

A. Building an Online Presence

Your online presence is the foundation of your marketing and promotion efforts. You can start by building a website that showcases your products, highlights your brand, and makes it easy for customers to shop online. Your website should be visually appealing, easy to navigate, and optimized for search engines. This will help you reach a wider audience and drive more traffic to your site.

B. Creating a Social Media Strategy

Social media is a powerful tool for reaching your target market and building your brand. By creating a strong presence on popular platforms like Instagram, Facebook, and Twitter, you can connect with customers, share your products and services, and build a community of loyal followers. Your social media strategy should include a mix of curated content, user-generated content, and product showcases to help you engage with your target audience and drive sales.

C. Running Marketing Campaigns

Marketing campaigns are a great way to reach a wider audience and generate interest in your products. You can run targeted ads on platforms like Facebook and Instagram, or participate in influencer marketing programs to reach customers who are interested in your products. Consider running seasonal promotions, like flash sales or holiday discounts, to drive sales and build excitement around your brand.

D. Building Relationships with Influencers

Influencer marketing is a powerful tool for reaching new customers and building your brand. By partnering with popular influencers in your industry, you can tap into their audiences and reach customers who are interested in your products. You can start by reaching out to influencers you admire, or participating in influencer marketing programs that connect you with influencers who are a good fit for your brand.

Marketing and promotion are ongoing efforts that require consistent effort and attention. By building a strong online presence, creating a social media strategy, running targeted campaigns, and building relationships with influencers, you can reach your target market, generate sales, and grow your online fashion business. With hard work and dedication, you can turn your vision into a thriving fashion brand!

CHAPTER SIX

Growing Your Business

You've successfully launched your online fashion business and now it's time to start growing it. Whether you're looking to expand your product line, improve customer service, or reach new customers, there are many strategies you can use to take your business to the next level.

A. Expanding Your Product Line

One of the easiest ways to grow your business is by expanding your product line. This can include adding new styles or categories of clothing, introducing accessories or footwear, or launching a line of beauty or grooming products. When expanding your product line, it's important to stay true to your brand and offer products that complement your existing line. You should also consider customer demand and feedback, and test new products before launching them on a larger scale.

B. Improving Customer Service

Customer service is a critical aspect of any business, and it's especially important in the world of online fashion. By providing excellent customer service, you can build a loyal customer base and foster positive relationships with your customers. This can include responding promptly to customer inquiries, offering easy returns and exchanges, and providing tracking information for shipments. You should also consider offering an online chat feature or phone support to help customers with questions or concerns.

C. Offering Sales and Promotions

Another way to grow your business is by offering sales and promotions. This can include discounts, free shipping, or special offers for new customers. You can promote these offers through your website, email marketing campaigns, or social media. It's important to strike a balance between offering promotions that attract new customers and maintaining the profitability of your business.

D. Growing Your Online Community

Finally, growing your online community is a great way to reach new customers and build brand awareness. This can include building a strong social media presence, engaging with customers and influencers on social media, and creating a loyalty program that rewards customers for their repeat business. You should also consider hosting events or product launches to engage with your customers in person and build relationships with the fashion community.

In conclusion, growing your business is an exciting part of the entrepreneurial journey. By expanding your product line, improving customer service, offering sales and promotions, and growing your online community, you can take your business to the next level and reach new customers. Remember, growth takes time and effort, but with persistence and dedication, you can achieve the success you're striving for.

CHAPTER SEVEN

Conclusion

Congratulations! You've made it to the end of this guide and you're one step closer to launching your online fashion business. By following the steps outlined in this guide, you have the foundation in place to build a successful and sustainable business.

A. Reflecting on Your Journey

Take a moment to reflect on your journey so far. What have you learned? What challenges have you faced? What have been some of your biggest successes? This reflection will help you understand what you've accomplished and where you still have room to grow.

B. Moving Forward with Confidence

Now that you have a strong foundation, it's time to move forward with confidence. Remember, starting a business is not easy, but with hard work and determination, you can achieve your goals. Stay focused on your mission and keep working towards your vision. Surround yourself with supportive people who will encourage you and help you succeed.

C. Final Thoughts on Launching an Online Fashion Business

Starting an online fashion business can be a rewarding and exciting journey. With the right tools and resources, you can turn your passion for fashion into a thriving business. Keep in mind that success takes time and patience, so don't be discouraged if you encounter challenges along the way. Embrace the learning process, and use your experiences to grow and improve.

We hope this guide has provided you with the information and inspiration you need to launch your online fashion business. Remember, success is possible with the right strategy, hard work, and determination. We wish you all the best in your new venture!

CHAPTER EIGHT

References and Resources

Congratulations on reaching the final chapter of this guide! By now, you should have a clear understanding of what it takes to launch a successful online fashion business. To help you continue your journey, this chapter will provide you with a list of resources and references to help you grow and succeed.

Recommended Books and Websites

1. The Lean Startup by Eric Ries
2. The Fashion Entrepreneur: Start and Run Your Own Fashion Business by Hazel 9781845284874
3. How to Win Friends and Influence People by Dale Carnegie
4. Shopify Academy - https://www.shopify.com/academy
5. Magento U - https://u.magento.com/
6. Fashionista - https://fashionista.com/

Additional Tools and Resources for Entrepreneurs

1. Canva - https://www.canva.com/
2. Hootsuite - https://hootsuite.com/
3. Mailchimp - https://mailchimp.com/
4. Google Analytics - https://analytics.google.com/

5. Shopify App Store - https://apps.shopify.com/

Glossary of Key Terms

1. E-commerce - the buying and selling of goods and services over the internet

2. Target Market - the specific group of consumers that a business wants to reach with its products or services

3. Business Plan - a written document that outlines a company's goals and strategies for achieving them

4. Brand - the unique identity of a company or product, including its name, logo, and visual appearance

5. Online Store - a website where customers can browse and purchase products

6. Marketing - the promotion of a product or service to potential customers

7. Social Media - websites and applications that allow users to create and share content or participate in social networking

We hope that this guide has been a valuable resource for you as you embark on your journey to launch your online fashion business. The world of fashion is constantly changing, and there will always be new challenges and opportunities to explore. With the information and resources provided in this guide, you'll be well-equipped to succeed. Best of luck on your entrepreneurial journey!

Printed by Libri Plureos GmbH in Hamburg,
Germany